PROJECT 2025

The Heritage Foundation's Mandate for Leadership and Its Impact on American Democracy Explained

Lila P. Katz

TABLE OF CONTENT

Introduction..5

    The Dawn of Project 2025 5

    Scope and Purpose of This Book 7

    Methodology and Sources 8

Chapter 1: The Historical Context 11

    Evolution of American Governance 11

    Key Political Milestones Leading to Project 2025...........14

    The Political Climate of the Early 2020s.........................17

Chapter 2: The Foundations of Project 2025 21

    Key Players and Influencers 21

    The Heritage Foundation's Mandate for Leadership..........23

    Underlying Philosophies and Objectives 26

Chapter 3: The Conservative Vision for America's Future.....29

    Core Conservative Principles..29

    Policy Proposals and Their Implications 32

    Balancing Tradition and Innovation...............................37

Chapter 4: Democracy at a Crossroads 40

    Challenges to Modern Democracy 40

    The Role of Public Opinion and Media...........................43

    Safeguarding Democratic Institutions 47

Chapter 5: Economic Policies Under Project 2025.................52

    Tax Reforms and Fiscal Policies.....................................52

    Economic Growth Strategies 55

    Impact on Various Sectors 59

Chapter 6: Social Policies and Their Impact........................64

Education and Healthcare Reforms 64

Social Justice and Equality Issues 68

The Future of Social Security and Welfare 72

Chapter 7: Foreign Policy and National Security 75

Project 2025's Global Vision 75

Defense Strategies and Military Readiness...................78

Diplomatic Presence...83

Chapter 8: Environmental and Energy Policies 87

Approaches to Climate Change 87

Energy Independence and Sustainability 90

Balancing Economic Growth with Environmental Protection...93

Chapter 9: The Public Response 97

Reactions from Different Political Spectrums.................97

Public Opinion and Grassroots Movements.................101

Chapter 10: The Path Forward 107

Potential Challenges and Opportunities 107

Long-Term Vision and Goals....................................111

Conclusion: The Future of Democracy and Leadership in America 114

Conclusion 118

Introduction

The Dawn of Project 2025

The landscape of American politics has always been in a state of flux, shaped by dynamic forces and ever-changing ideologies. However, the emergence of Project 2025 marks a pivotal moment in the nation's journey. This initiative, born out of a desire to reshape the governance of the United States, has garnered significant attention and sparked intense debate across the political spectrum. As we stand at the threshold of this ambitious endeavor, it is crucial to understand its origins, motivations, and potential implications for the future of American democracy.

Project 2025 was conceived in response to a growing sense of dissatisfaction with the status quo. A coalition of conservative thinkers, policy experts, and political leaders came together with a shared vision of revitalizing the American government. They sought to address what they perceived as systemic issues that had plagued the nation for decades, from economic stagnation to social divisions. This coalition believed that a bold and comprehensive approach was necessary to steer the country toward a more prosperous and unified future.

At the heart of Project 2025 lies the Heritage Foundation's Mandate for Leadership. This document serves as the blueprint for the initiative, outlining a series of policy proposals aimed at overhauling various aspects of government and society. From tax reforms to healthcare policy, the Mandate for Leadership provides a detailed roadmap for implementing conservative principles in governance. The Heritage Foundation, a prominent conservative think tank, has played a central role in shaping and promoting this vision.

The timing of Project 2025 is not coincidental. The political climate of the early 2020s has been characterized by heightened polarization and a growing divide between conservative and liberal ideologies. The 2024 presidential election, which saw a fierce contest between incumbent President Joe Biden and former President Donald Trump, further underscored the deep-seated divisions within the country. In the wake of this contentious election, the proponents of Project 2025 saw an opportunity to seize the moment and push for transformative change.

However, the initiative has not been without its critics. Opponents argue that Project 2025 represents a radical shift that threatens to undermine key democratic institutions and values. They caution against the potential consequences of implementing such sweeping changes, particularly in a political environment already fraught with tension and uncertainty. The debate surrounding Project 2025 has, in many ways, become a microcosm of the broader struggle over the direction of American governance and society.

Scope and Purpose of This Book

This book aims to provide a comprehensive and balanced exploration of Project 2025. It seeks to dissect the initiative from multiple angles, offering readers a thorough understanding of its origins, objectives, and potential impact on the United States. By delving into the key components of the Heritage Foundation's Mandate for Leadership, we will examine the specific policy proposals and their implications for various sectors of society.

One of the primary goals of this book is to foster informed discussion and critical thinking about Project 2025. In an era where political discourse is often dominated by sound bites and superficial analysis, it is essential to take a deeper dive into the complexities of this initiative. Through meticulous research and thoughtful analysis, we aim to present a nuanced perspective that goes beyond partisan rhetoric.

The book is structured to guide readers through the intricate web of issues related to Project 2025. Each chapter focuses on a distinct aspect of the initiative, from its historical context to its economic and social policies. By breaking down these components, we hope to provide a clear and coherent narrative that illuminates the broader implications of Project 2025 for American democracy.

In addition to exploring the specifics of the initiative, this book also aims to situate Project 2025 within the broader context of American political history. By tracing the evolution of governance in the

United States, we can better understand the forces that have shaped the current political landscape and the motivations behind the push for change. This historical perspective is crucial for grasping the significance of Project 2025 and its potential impact on the future of the nation.

Ultimately, the purpose of this book is not to advocate for or against Project 2025. Rather, it is to provide readers with the information and insights needed to form their own opinions and engage in meaningful dialogue about the future of American governance. By presenting a balanced and well-researched account, we hope to contribute to a more informed and engaged citizenry.

Methodology and Sources

The research and analysis presented in this book are grounded in a rigorous and systematic approach. Our methodology combines qualitative and quantitative research methods to ensure a comprehensive and accurate portrayal of Project 2025. This approach allows us to capture the complexity of the initiative and provide readers with a well-rounded understanding of its various dimensions.

One of the primary sources of information for this book is the Heritage Foundation's Mandate for Leadership. This document serves as the cornerstone of Project 2025, outlining the key policy proposals and guiding principles of the initiative. By closely examining the Mandate for Leadership, we can gain valuable insights into the vision and goals of Project 2025.

In addition to the Mandate for Leadership, this book draws on a wide range of secondary sources, including academic articles, policy papers, and news reports. These sources provide diverse perspectives on Project 2025 and help to contextualize the initiative within the broader landscape of American politics. By synthesizing information from multiple sources, we aim to present a balanced and well-informed analysis.

Interviews with key stakeholders and experts also play a crucial role in our research. By engaging with individuals who have direct knowledge and experience related to Project 2025, we can gain deeper insights into the motivations, challenges, and potential impact of the initiative. These interviews provide firsthand accounts and expert opinions that enrich our understanding of the subject matter.

Furthermore, this book incorporates data and statistical analysis to support our findings and arguments. By examining relevant data on economic indicators, social trends, and public opinion, we can provide evidence-based insights into the potential consequences of Project 2025. This quantitative approach complements our qualitative analysis and adds depth to our exploration of the initiative.

Throughout the research process, we have adhered to the highest standards of academic integrity and ethical conduct. All sources are meticulously cited, and efforts have been made to ensure the accuracy and reliability of the information presented. By maintaining a commitment to rigorous research practices, we aim to provide readers with a trustworthy and credible account of Project 2025.

In conclusion, the methodology and sources used in this book reflect a commitment to thorough and balanced research. By combining qualitative and quantitative approaches, engaging with diverse perspectives, and adhering to ethical standards, we aim to present a comprehensive and well-rounded exploration of Project 2025. This book is intended to serve as a valuable resource for anyone seeking to understand the future of American democracy and the potential impact of this ambitious initiative.

Chapter 1: The Historical Context

Evolution of American Governance

The story of American governance is a tale of continuous evolution, shaped by a myriad of influences and events over centuries. The founding of the United States was marked by a revolutionary break from colonial rule and the establishment of a republic grounded in democratic ideals. The framers of the Constitution envisioned a system of government that balanced power among the executive, legislative, and judicial branches, ensuring no single entity could dominate the others. This framework, while robust, was designed to be adaptable, allowing for amendments and interpretations that would enable the nation to address emerging challenges and changing societal values.

From the ratification of the Constitution in 1788, American governance has undergone significant transformations. The early years were characterized by the development of foundational institutions and practices, including the creation of the Bill of Rights, which enshrined essential liberties and protections for citizens. The young republic faced numerous tests, including the War of 1812, which solidified the nation's sovereignty and demonstrated its resilience.

The 19th century brought about profound changes, including the expansion westward, which was driven by the concept of Manifest Destiny. This period saw the incorporation of new territories and states, altering the political landscape and raising contentious issues such as slavery. The Civil War (1861-1865) was a pivotal moment, testing the limits of federalism and the principles of democracy. The post-war Reconstruction era sought to redefine the nation's values and integrate formerly enslaved individuals into the political and social fabric of the country.

The turn of the 20th century ushered in the Progressive Era, marked by a wave of reforms aimed at addressing the excesses of industrialization and improving social welfare. Leaders like Theodore Roosevelt championed regulatory measures to curb corporate power and protect workers' rights. This period also saw significant advancements in women's suffrage, culminating in the 19th Amendment in 1920, which granted women the right to vote.

The Great Depression of the 1930s prompted another transformation in American governance, with the New Deal policies of Franklin D. Roosevelt expanding the role of the federal government in economic and social affairs. These measures aimed to provide relief, recovery, and reform to a nation in crisis, laying the groundwork for the modern welfare state. The post-World War II era saw further expansions in federal power, particularly in areas such as civil rights, healthcare, and education.

The latter half of the 20th century was characterized by a series of ideological shifts and policy debates. The Civil Rights Movement of the 1960s led to landmark legislation, including the Civil Rights Act of 1964 and the Voting Rights Act of 1965, which sought to dismantle systemic racism and ensure equal protection under the law. The Vietnam War and the Watergate scandal of the 1970s prompted a reevaluation of executive power and led to increased demands for transparency and accountability in government.

The 1980s brought a conservative resurgence under President Ronald Reagan, who advocated for limited government, deregulation, and tax cuts. This era emphasized free-market principles and sought to roll back many of the regulatory frameworks established during the New Deal and Great Society programs. The end of the Cold War in the early 1990s marked a significant geopolitical shift, with the United States emerging as the world's sole superpower.

As the 21st century dawned, the United States faced new challenges and opportunities. The terrorist attacks of September 11, 2001, reshaped national security policies and led to the establishment of the Department of Homeland Security. The subsequent wars in Afghanistan and Iraq had profound implications for foreign policy and military strategy. Domestically, the Great Recession of 2008 prompted significant economic interventions, including the Troubled Asset Relief Program (TARP) and the American Recovery and Reinvestment Act.

Throughout these epochs, American governance has continually adapted to meet the needs of its citizens and address the complexities of a changing world. The emergence of Project 2025 can be seen as part of this ongoing evolution, reflecting contemporary debates about the role of government, the balance of power, and the future direction of the nation.

Key Political Milestones Leading to Project 2025

The journey to Project 2025 is paved with numerous political milestones that have shaped the current landscape. These events, movements, and decisions have collectively contributed to the conditions that necessitated a rethinking of American governance.

One of the most significant milestones was the 2016 presidential election, which brought Donald Trump to the White House. Trump's victory was a seismic event in American politics, signaling a shift toward populism and a rejection of established political norms. His administration pursued an agenda centered on deregulation, tax cuts, and a strong stance on immigration. The Trump presidency also underscored deep divisions within the American electorate, with stark contrasts between urban and rural areas, as well as between different demographic groups.

The 2016 election was also notable for its impact on the judiciary. President Trump appointed three Supreme Court justices, significantly altering the ideological balance of the Court. These appointments, along with numerous lower court judges, have had and will continue to have long-lasting effects on American law and policy.

The 2020 presidential election, held amid the COVID-19 pandemic, was another pivotal moment. The election saw a record voter turnout and resulted in the victory of Joe Biden, who campaigned on a platform of unity, pandemic response, and economic recovery. The election was marred by allegations of fraud and subsequent challenges to the results, culminating in the unprecedented storming of the U.S. Capitol on January 6, 2021. This event highlighted the fragility of democratic institutions and the deep-seated divisions within the country.

In the years following the 2020 election, several states enacted significant changes to their voting laws. These changes, often framed as measures to enhance election security, have been criticized by opponents as efforts to suppress voter turnout, particularly among minority groups. The debate over voting rights has become a central issue in the broader conversation about democracy and governance.

Another key milestone was the confirmation of Justice Amy Coney Barrett to the Supreme Court in October 2020, just weeks before the presidential election. Barrett's confirmation cemented a conservative majority on the Court, which has since issued rulings with far-reaching implications for issues such as abortion, gun rights, and religious freedom. The judiciary's role in shaping policy has become increasingly prominent, reflecting the significance of judicial appointments in contemporary politics.

The economic and social upheavals of the early 2020s also played a crucial role in shaping the political landscape. The COVID-19 pandemic exposed and exacerbated existing inequalities, prompting calls for comprehensive healthcare reform and increased social safety nets. The pandemic also accelerated shifts in the labor market, with remote work and technological advancements transforming industries and employment patterns.

In response to these challenges, the Biden administration pursued ambitious policy initiatives, including the American Rescue Plan and the Infrastructure Investment and Jobs Act. These measures aimed to provide economic relief, create jobs, and modernize critical infrastructure. However, they also sparked debates about the appropriate level of government intervention and fiscal responsibility.

Amid these developments, conservative thinkers and policymakers began to articulate a vision for the future that would later coalesce into Project 2025. The Heritage Foundation's Mandate for Leadership, first published in the 1980s, served as a foundational document for this vision. The Mandate outlined a comprehensive agenda for conservative governance, emphasizing limited government, free-market principles, and a strong national defense.

The publication of subsequent editions of the Mandate for Leadership, particularly in the lead-up to presidential elections, reflected the evolving priorities and strategies of the conservative movement. These documents provided a blueprint for policy proposals and legislative initiatives that sought to reshape American governance in line with conservative principles.

The convergence of these political milestones set the stage for the formal announcement of Project 2025. The initiative aimed to build on the successes and lessons of previous conservative efforts, addressing contemporary challenges while adhering to core principles. The goal was to present a cohesive and compelling vision for the future of American governance, one that could resonate with a broad coalition of voters and policymakers.

The Political Climate of the Early 2020s

The early 2020s were marked by a highly polarized and contentious political climate. The aftermath of the 2020 presidential election, characterized by allegations of fraud and the events of January 6, 2021, exacerbated divisions within the country. Trust in institutions, including the media, government, and judiciary, reached historic lows, contributing to an environment of heightened skepticism and partisanship.

One of the defining features of this period was the stark ideological divide between conservative and liberal perspectives. Issues such as healthcare, immigration, climate change, and social justice became flashpoints for intense debate and activism. The rise of movements like Black Lives Matter and the response to police violence highlighted deep-seated racial and social inequalities, prompting widespread calls for reform.

Economic disparities also played a significant role in shaping the political climate. The COVID-19 pandemic exposed vulnerabilities in the healthcare system and labor market, with disproportionate impacts on low-income and minority communities. The economic fallout prompted discussions about the need for robust social safety nets and measures to address income inequality.

The Biden administration's policy agenda reflected these priorities, with significant investments in infrastructure, healthcare, and social programs. However, these initiatives faced staunch opposition from conservative lawmakers, who argued that such spending was fiscally irresponsible and risked expanding the role of government beyond acceptable limits. This ideological clash underscored the broader debate about the direction of American governance and the balance between federal and state power.

The cultural landscape of the early 2020s was also characterized by a heightened focus on identity and representation. Issues related to gender, sexuality, and racial equity dominated public discourse, influencing policy decisions and societal norms. The confirmation of the first female and first African American Vice President, Kamala Harris, was a historic milestone that reflected broader trends toward diversity and inclusion in American politics.

Amid these cultural and economic shifts, the conservative movement sought to articulate a coherent vision for the future. Project 2025 emerged as a response to these challenges, offering a roadmap for addressing contemporary issues through the lens of conservative principles. The initiative aimed to provide solutions that balanced economic growth with fiscal responsibility, national security with individual liberties, and social cohesion with respect for diverse perspectives.

The political climate of the early 2020s also saw significant changes in the media landscape. The proliferation of social media and digital platforms transformed how information was disseminated and consumed, contributing to the spread of misinformation and the erosion of traditional gatekeepers. This shift had profound implications for political communication and public opinion, with algorithms and echo chambers influencing the way individuals engaged with political content.

In this environment, the role of grassroots movements and community organizations became increasingly important. Activists and advocacy groups mobilized around key issues, leveraging digital tools to amplify their voices and effect change. The rise of these movements reflected a broader trend toward decentralized and participatory forms of political engagement, challenging traditional hierarchies and power structures.

The convergence of these factors created a complex and dynamic political landscape, one that required careful navigation and strategic thinking. Project 2025 sought to address these challenges by presenting a vision that was both forward-looking and rooted in established principles. The initiative aimed to provide a framework for governance that could adapt to changing conditions while maintaining a commitment to core values.

As we explore the historical context of Project 2025, it is essential to recognize the interplay of these various influences and how they have shaped the current moment. The evolution of American governance, the key political milestones, and the unique climate of the early 2020s all contribute to our understanding of this initiative and its potential impact on the future of the United States.

Chapter 2: The Foundations of Project 2025

Key Players and Influencers

The conception and promotion of Project 2025 have been driven by a diverse group of individuals and organizations, each playing a significant role in shaping its vision and objectives. Understanding the key players and influencers involved provides critical insight into the initiative's foundations and the motivations behind it.

The Heritage Foundation

At the forefront of Project 2025 is the Heritage Foundation, a prominent conservative think tank known for its influential policy research and advocacy. Established in 1973, the Heritage Foundation has long been a powerhouse in the conservative movement, providing policymakers with research and recommendations across a broad spectrum of issues, including economics, national security, and social policy.

The Heritage Foundation's involvement in Project 2025 is a natural extension of its historical mission. The organization has consistently championed principles of limited government, free enterprise, individual freedom, traditional values, and a strong national defense. These core values underpin the policy proposals laid out in the

Mandate for Leadership, the document that serves as the blueprint for Project 2025.

Key Individuals

Kay Coles James - As the President of the Heritage Foundation during the early phases of Project 2025, Kay Coles James played a pivotal role in steering the initiative. Her leadership emphasized the importance of returning to fundamental conservative principles while addressing contemporary challenges facing the nation.

Edwin J. Feulner - A co-founder of the Heritage Foundation, Edwin J. Feulner has been a driving force behind the organization's strategic direction. His vision of a robust conservative agenda continues to influence the framework of Project 2025.

Jim DeMint - A former U.S. Senator and President of the Heritage Foundation, Jim DeMint's tenure saw an emphasis on grassroots mobilization and policy advocacy. His efforts in promoting conservative policies have significantly shaped the discourse around Project 2025.

Political Leaders and Lawmakers

Project 2025 has garnered support from numerous conservative political leaders and lawmakers who see the initiative as a pathway to achieving long-standing policy goals. Key figures include:

Senator Tom Cotton - Known for his strong stance on national security and conservative values, Senator Tom Cotton has been an outspoken advocate for many of the principles outlined in the Mandate for Leadership. His legislative efforts often align with the goals of Project 2025.

Representative Jim Jordan - As a leading figure in the House Freedom Caucus, Representative Jim Jordan's commitment to limited government and fiscal conservatism resonates with the objectives of Project 2025. His advocacy for conservative policies has been instrumental in garnering support for the initiative.

Senator Marsha Blackburn - Senator Marsha Blackburn's focus on economic freedom, healthcare reform, and family values aligns closely with the priorities of Project 2025. Her legislative work and public advocacy have helped to promote the initiative's goals.

The Heritage Foundation's Mandate for Leadership

The Mandate for Leadership is a comprehensive policy document that serves as the foundation for Project 2025. First published in 1981 during the Reagan administration, the Mandate has been updated and revised to address contemporary issues and provide a roadmap for conservative governance. The document covers a wide range of policy areas, offering detailed recommendations and strategies for implementation.

Historical Context

The original Mandate for Leadership was a groundbreaking document that provided the incoming Reagan administration with a detailed policy agenda. Its success in shaping the administration's policies and priorities cemented the Heritage Foundation's reputation as a leading policy influencer. Subsequent editions of the Mandate have continued to reflect the evolving priorities of the conservative movement, adapting to new challenges and opportunities.

Key Components

The Mandate for Leadership is organized into several key areas, each addressing critical aspects of governance and policy. These areas include:

Economic Policy - The Mandate emphasizes the importance of free-market principles, advocating for tax cuts, deregulation, and policies that promote economic growth and innovation. It calls for fiscal responsibility and measures to reduce government spending and debt.

National Security - The document outlines a robust national defense strategy, emphasizing the need for a strong military, secure borders, and proactive measures to address emerging threats. It advocates for increased defense spending and policies that ensure America's security and global leadership.

Healthcare - The Mandate proposes reforms to the healthcare system aimed at increasing competition, reducing costs, and expanding access to quality care. It calls for the repeal of the Affordable Care Act and the implementation of market-based solutions.

Education - The document advocates for school choice, including vouchers and charter schools, as a means to improve educational outcomes and empower parents. It emphasizes the need for accountability and standards in education.

Social Policy - The Mandate addresses issues related to family values, religious freedom, and the sanctity of life. It calls for policies that protect traditional values and promote the well-being of families.

Energy and Environment - The document advocates for policies that promote energy independence and economic growth, including the development of domestic energy resources and the reduction of regulatory barriers. It emphasizes the importance of balancing environmental protection with economic considerations.

Underlying Philosophies and Objectives

The philosophies and objectives underlying Project 2025 are rooted in the core principles of conservatism, reflecting a commitment to limited government, individual liberty, free enterprise, and strong national defense. These principles guide the policy proposals and strategic direction of the initiative.

Limited Government

A central tenet of Project 2025 is the belief in limited government. The initiative advocates for a reduction in the size and scope of the federal government, arguing that excessive government intervention stifles economic growth, infringes on individual freedoms, and leads to inefficiencies. By promoting policies that devolve power to state and local governments, Project 2025 seeks to empower communities and individuals to make decisions that best meet their needs.

Individual Liberty

The protection of individual liberty is a cornerstone of Project 2025. The initiative emphasizes the importance of safeguarding constitutional rights, including freedom of speech, religious freedom, and the right to bear arms. It advocates for policies that protect these liberties from government overreach and ensure that individuals can live their lives according to their values and beliefs.

Free Enterprise

Economic freedom is another key pillar of Project 2025. The initiative promotes free-market principles, arguing that competition and innovation drive economic growth and improve living standards. By advocating for tax cuts, deregulation, and policies that support entrepreneurship, Project 2025 aims to create an environment where businesses can thrive and individuals can achieve economic success.

Strong National Defense

Project 2025 underscores the importance of a strong national defense to protect America's interests and ensure its security. The initiative advocates for increased defense spending, modernization of the military, and proactive measures to address emerging threats. It emphasizes the need for a robust national security strategy that includes secure borders, intelligence capabilities, and international alliances.

Social and Cultural Values

The initiative also places a strong emphasis on preserving traditional social and cultural values. It advocates for policies that protect the sanctity of life, promote family well-being, and uphold religious freedom. Project 2025 seeks to create a society that respects and values diverse perspectives while maintaining a commitment to core principles and ethical standards.

The foundations of Project 2025 are deeply rooted in the principles and philosophies of conservatism, shaped by the efforts of key players and influencers who have dedicated their careers to advancing these values. The Heritage Foundation's Mandate for Leadership provides a comprehensive roadmap for achieving the initiative's goals, offering detailed policy proposals across a wide range of areas. By understanding the underlying philosophies and objectives of Project 2025, we can better appreciate the vision and ambition of this initiative and its potential impact on the future of American governance.

Chapter 3: The Conservative Vision for America's Future

Core Conservative Principles

The conservative vision for America's future is grounded in a set of core principles that have guided the movement for decades. These principles reflect a commitment to limited government, individual liberty, free enterprise, strong national defense, and the preservation of traditional values. By adhering to these foundational beliefs, conservatives aim to promote a society that is both prosperous and just, where individuals are free to pursue their goals and where government interference is minimized.

Limited Government

One of the most fundamental principles of conservatism is the belief in limited government. Conservatives argue that government should play a minimal role in the lives of citizens, intervening only when absolutely necessary. This principle is rooted in a deep skepticism of centralized power, which is seen as inherently prone to corruption and inefficiency. By limiting the scope of government, conservatives believe that individual freedoms can be better protected, and that innovation and economic growth can flourish.

The conservative vision for limited government involves reducing federal spending, eliminating unnecessary regulations, and devolving power to state and local governments. By decentralizing authority, conservatives aim to empower communities and individuals to make decisions that best reflect their needs and values. This approach is seen as a way to foster greater accountability and responsiveness in governance.

Individual Liberty

The protection of individual liberty is another cornerstone of conservative philosophy. Conservatives believe that individuals should have the freedom to make their own choices and live their lives according to their values and beliefs. This principle encompasses a wide range of rights, including freedom of speech, religious freedom, and the right to bear arms. Conservatives argue that these liberties are essential to the functioning of a free and democratic society.

To safeguard individual liberty, conservatives advocate for a strict interpretation of the Constitution, emphasizing the importance of the Bill of Rights and other constitutional protections. They oppose government overreach and support policies that limit the power of the state to infringe upon personal freedoms. This commitment to individual liberty is seen as a way to ensure that citizens can pursue their dreams and aspirations without undue interference.

Free Enterprise

Economic freedom is a key pillar of conservative thought. Conservatives believe that free-market principles drive innovation, create wealth, and improve living standards. They argue that competition and entrepreneurship are the engines of economic growth, and that government intervention often stifles these forces. By promoting policies that support free enterprise, conservatives aim to create an environment where businesses can thrive and individuals can achieve economic success.

The conservative vision for economic policy includes tax cuts, deregulation, and measures to reduce the size of government. Conservatives advocate for lower taxes as a way to stimulate investment and job creation, arguing that individuals and businesses are better equipped to allocate resources than the government. Deregulation is seen as a way to remove barriers to innovation and reduce the costs of compliance for businesses.

Strong National Defense

A strong national defense is central to the conservative vision for America's future. Conservatives believe that the primary role of government is to protect the nation's security and ensure its sovereignty. This principle involves maintaining a robust military, securing the nation's borders, and taking proactive measures to address emerging threats.

Conservatives argue that a strong national defense is essential to preserving peace and stability. They advocate for increased defense spending, the modernization of military capabilities, and the development of strategic alliances with other nations. By prioritizing national security, conservatives aim to ensure that America remains a global leader and can effectively respond to challenges in an increasingly complex world.

Preservation of Traditional Values

The preservation of traditional values is another key aspect of the conservative vision. Conservatives believe that cultural and moral values play a crucial role in shaping society and ensuring its stability. They argue that institutions such as the family, religion, and community are essential to fostering a sense of responsibility, respect, and social cohesion.

To preserve traditional values, conservatives advocate for policies that protect the sanctity of life, uphold religious freedom, and promote the well-being of families. They oppose efforts to redefine social institutions and argue that government should support, rather than undermine, the cultural and moral foundations of society.

Policy Proposals and Their Implications

The conservative vision for America's future is not just about principles; it is also about concrete policy proposals designed to translate these principles into action. These proposals cover a wide range of areas, from economic policy to healthcare, education, and national security. Each policy proposal is intended to promote conservative values while addressing the challenges facing the nation.

Economic Policy

One of the central elements of the conservative economic agenda is tax reform. Conservatives argue that the current tax system is overly complex and imposes a significant burden on individuals and businesses. They advocate for lower tax rates, simplification of the tax code, and measures to eliminate loopholes and deductions. The goal is to create a tax system that is fairer, more efficient, and more conducive to economic growth.

In addition to tax reform, conservatives support deregulation as a way to reduce the costs of doing business and promote innovation. They argue that excessive regulation stifles entrepreneurship and imposes unnecessary burdens on businesses. By rolling back regulations, conservatives believe that the economy can become more dynamic and competitive.

Another key aspect of the conservative economic agenda is fiscal responsibility. Conservatives advocate for measures to reduce government spending and address the national debt. They argue that unsustainable levels of debt pose a threat to the nation's economic stability and future prosperity. By prioritizing fiscal discipline, conservatives aim to ensure that government spending is aligned with the nation's long-term interests.

Healthcare

Healthcare is another area where conservatives have proposed significant reforms. Conservatives argue that the current healthcare system is plagued by inefficiencies and high costs, largely due to excessive government intervention. They advocate for market-based solutions that increase competition, reduce costs, and improve access to quality care.

One of the central proposals in the conservative healthcare agenda is the repeal and replacement of the Affordable Care Act (ACA). Conservatives argue that the ACA has led to higher premiums, reduced choices, and increased government control over healthcare. They propose replacing it with policies that promote competition among insurers, provide tax credits for individuals to purchase insurance, and allow for the sale of insurance across state lines.

In addition to these measures, conservatives support reforms to Medicare and Medicaid aimed at reducing costs and improving efficiency. They advocate for a shift toward premium support for Medicare, where beneficiaries receive a fixed amount to purchase insurance, and block grants for Medicaid, giving states more flexibility to design their programs.

Education

Education policy is another key area of focus for conservatives. They argue that the current education system is failing to provide students with the skills and knowledge they need to succeed in a rapidly changing world. Conservatives advocate for policies that promote school choice, increase accountability, and improve educational outcomes.

One of the central proposals in the conservative education agenda is the expansion of school choice programs, including vouchers, charter schools, and education savings accounts. Conservatives argue that giving parents the ability to choose the best educational options for their children will lead to improved outcomes and greater innovation in education.

In addition to school choice, conservatives support measures to increase accountability in education. They advocate for rigorous standards and assessments, performance-based pay for teachers, and greater transparency in school performance. By holding schools accountable for results, conservatives believe that the education system can be improved and that students can receive a better education.

National Security

National security is a top priority for conservatives, and their policy proposals reflect a commitment to maintaining a strong and capable military. Conservatives argue that the world is becoming increasingly dangerous, with threats ranging from terrorism to cyberattacks, and that the United States must be prepared to defend itself and its interests.

One of the central elements of the conservative national security agenda is increased defense spending. Conservatives argue that the military has been underfunded in recent years and that significant investments are needed to modernize and strengthen the armed forces. This includes investments in advanced technologies, such as missile defense systems, cyber capabilities, and space-based assets.

In addition to defense spending, conservatives support policies to enhance border security and immigration enforcement. They argue that secure borders are essential to national security and that immigration laws must be enforced to protect the nation's sovereignty. This includes measures to build physical barriers, increase the number of border patrol agents, and enhance the use of technology for surveillance and enforcement.

Social Policy

Social policy is another area where conservatives have proposed significant reforms. Conservatives argue that traditional values and cultural norms play a crucial role in shaping society and that government policies should support, rather than undermine, these values.

One of the central elements of the conservative social policy agenda is the protection of life. Conservatives advocate for policies that restrict access to abortion and promote alternatives, such as adoption. They argue that protecting the sanctity of life is a moral imperative and that government policies should reflect this commitment.

In addition to the protection of life, conservatives support policies that uphold religious freedom and protect the rights of individuals to practice their faith. This includes measures to ensure that religious institutions and individuals are not compelled to act against their beliefs, as well as policies that protect religious expression in the public square.

Balancing Tradition and Innovation

One of the key challenges for conservatives is finding the right balance between tradition and innovation. While conservatism is rooted in a respect for tradition and a commitment to preserving core values, it also recognizes the need for progress and adaptation in response to changing circumstances.

Preserving Core Values

Conservatives believe that certain values and principles are timeless and that they provide a foundation for a stable and prosperous society. These core values include respect for individual liberty, the rule of law, and the importance of family and community. By preserving these values, conservatives argue that society can maintain a sense of continuity and stability in the face of change.

To preserve core values, conservatives advocate for policies that protect individual rights, uphold the Constitution, and promote the well-being of families and communities. They argue that government should support, rather than undermine, these values, and that public policy should reflect a commitment to preserving the cultural and moral foundations of society.

Embracing Innovation

While conservatism is rooted in a respect for tradition, it also recognizes the need for innovation and progress. Conservatives argue that society must adapt to changing circumstances and that innovation is essential to addressing new challenges and seizing new opportunities.

In the realm of economic policy, conservatives support measures that promote innovation and entrepreneurship. This includes policies that reduce regulatory barriers, encourage investment in research and development, and support the growth of new industries. By fostering a dynamic and competitive economy, conservatives believe that the United States can maintain its global leadership and ensure long-term prosperity.

In the realm of national security, conservatives recognize the need to adapt to emerging threats and technologies. This includes investments in advanced military capabilities, such as cyber defense and space-based assets, as well as measures to enhance intelligence and surveillance capabilities. By staying ahead of potential adversaries, conservatives argue that the United States can better protect its interests and ensure its security.

Integrating Tradition and Innovation

The conservative vision for America's future involves integrating tradition and innovation in a way that respects core values while embracing progress. This approach recognizes that tradition and innovation are not mutually exclusive, but rather complementary forces that can work together to create a better society.

One example of this integration is in the area of education policy. Conservatives advocate for policies that promote school choice and innovation in education, while also emphasizing the importance of accountability and standards. By giving parents more options and encouraging innovation, conservatives believe that the education system can be improved, while also ensuring that students receive a high-quality education that prepares them for the future.

Another example is in the area of healthcare policy. Conservatives support market-based solutions that promote competition and innovation, while also emphasizing the importance of protecting individual rights and ensuring access to quality care. By encouraging innovation in healthcare, conservatives believe that the system can become more efficient and effective, while also respecting the principles of individual liberty and limited government.

Chapter 4: Democracy at a Crossroads

Challenges to Modern Democracy

Modern democracy faces a myriad of challenges that threaten its stability and effectiveness. These challenges are multifaceted, encompassing political, economic, social, and technological dimensions. Understanding these challenges is crucial for developing strategies to safeguard and strengthen democratic institutions.

Political Polarization

One of the most significant challenges to modern democracy is political polarization. In recent years, the ideological divide between conservatives and liberals has widened, leading to increased partisanship and gridlock in government. This polarization is often fueled by social and traditional media, which can amplify extreme views and create echo chambers where individuals are only exposed to information that reinforces their existing beliefs.

The consequences of political polarization are profound. It can lead to legislative paralysis, where important policy decisions are delayed or obstructed due to partisan conflict. Polarization also undermines trust in government and erodes the social fabric, as individuals become more likely to view those with opposing views as enemies rather than fellow citizens. This environment makes it difficult to achieve consensus on critical issues and weakens the overall functioning of democratic institutions.

Economic Inequality

Economic inequality poses another significant challenge to modern democracy. When a small segment of the population holds a disproportionate share of wealth and resources, it can lead to social and political instability. Economic disparities can undermine the principle of equal representation, as those with greater financial means often have more influence over the political process through campaign contributions, lobbying, and other means.

The growing gap between the rich and the poor can also erode social cohesion and fuel populist movements that exploit economic grievances. These movements often promise simple solutions to complex problems, appealing to individuals who feel left behind by the current system. The result can be a cycle of political instability and policy swings that make it difficult to address long-term challenges effectively.

Disinformation and Misinformation

The spread of disinformation and misinformation is a critical threat to modern democracy. In the digital age, false information can spread rapidly through social media and other online platforms, often reaching millions of people before it can be corrected.

Disinformation campaigns, whether domestic or foreign, can manipulate public opinion, undermine trust in institutions, and influence electoral outcomes.

The proliferation of false information creates an environment where it is increasingly difficult for citizens to discern fact from fiction. This erodes trust in traditional sources of information, such as the media and government, and can lead to widespread cynicism and disengagement from the political process. Addressing the challenge of disinformation requires a multifaceted approach that includes media literacy, regulation of social media platforms, and efforts to promote credible sources of information.

Decline in Civic Engagement

A decline in civic engagement poses another challenge to modern democracy. Civic engagement, which includes activities such as voting, volunteering, and participating in community organizations, is essential for the health of democratic societies. When citizens are actively involved in the political process, they can hold their representatives accountable and contribute to the development of policies that reflect the public's needs and values.

However, many democracies have seen a decline in civic engagement, particularly among younger generations. This disengagement can be attributed to various factors, including disillusionment with the political system, lack of trust in institutions, and a feeling that individual actions do not make a difference. The decline in civic engagement weakens the connection between citizens and their government, making it more difficult to address collective challenges and build a sense of shared purpose.

Erosion of Democratic Norms

The erosion of democratic norms is another critical challenge facing modern democracies. Democratic norms, such as respect for the rule of law, the peaceful transfer of power, and the protection of minority rights, are the unwritten rules that support the functioning of democratic institutions. When these norms are undermined, it can lead to a breakdown in democratic governance and the rise of authoritarian tendencies.

In recent years, there have been numerous examples of democratic norms being challenged or disregarded. These include efforts to undermine the independence of the judiciary, attempts to weaken checks and balances, and attacks on the free press. The erosion of democratic norms can create an environment where the rule of law is weakened, and the rights of individuals are not adequately protected.

The Role of Public Opinion and Media

Public opinion and media play a crucial role in shaping the dynamics of modern democracy. They influence how citizens perceive political issues, form their opinions, and make decisions about their participation in the political process. Understanding the interplay between public opinion, media, and democracy is essential for addressing the challenges facing democratic societies.

Shaping Public Opinion

Public opinion is the aggregate of individual attitudes and beliefs about political issues, leaders, and institutions. It is shaped by various factors, including personal experiences, cultural background, education, and exposure to media. Public opinion can influence policy decisions, electoral outcomes, and the overall direction of a country.

Media plays a significant role in shaping public opinion by providing information, framing issues, and setting the agenda for public discourse. Traditional media, such as newspapers, television, and radio, have historically been the primary sources of news and information. However, the rise of digital media has transformed the media landscape, with social media platforms, blogs, and online news outlets becoming increasingly influential.

The Influence of Traditional Media

Traditional media outlets have long been seen as gatekeepers of information, responsible for ensuring that news is accurate, balanced, and fair. They play a critical role in informing the public, holding government officials accountable, and providing a forum for public debate. In democratic societies, a free and independent press is considered essential for the functioning of democracy.

However, traditional media faces several challenges that impact its ability to fulfill these roles. Economic pressures, changes in consumer behavior, and competition from digital media have led to the decline of many traditional news organizations. Additionally, concerns about media bias and the concentration of media ownership have raised questions about the diversity and quality of information available to the public.

The Rise of Digital Media

The rise of digital media has transformed how people consume news and information. Social media platforms, such as Facebook, Twitter, and Instagram, allow individuals to access and share information instantaneously. Online news outlets and blogs provide alternative sources of news, often catering to specific audiences and perspectives.

While digital media has democratized access to information, it has also contributed to the spread of disinformation and the creation of echo chambers. Algorithms used by social media platforms often prioritize content that generates engagement, which can lead to the amplification of sensational or misleading information. This environment can make it challenging for individuals to find accurate and reliable information and can contribute to the polarization of public opinion.

Media Literacy and Critical Thinking

In an era of information overload, media literacy and critical thinking skills are essential for navigating the complex media landscape. Media literacy involves the ability to access, analyze, evaluate, and create media in various forms. It empowers individuals to make informed decisions about the information they consume and share.

Promoting media literacy requires efforts from educators, media organizations, and policymakers. Educational programs can help individuals develop the skills needed to critically evaluate information, recognize bias, and distinguish between credible sources and disinformation. Media organizations can contribute by providing transparency about their sources and methods and by promoting ethical journalism.

The Role of Public Opinion in Democracy

Public opinion plays a vital role in democratic governance. In a democracy, elected officials are accountable to the people and must be responsive to their constituents' views and concerns. Public opinion can influence policy decisions, shape electoral outcomes, and hold government officials accountable.

However, the relationship between public opinion and policy is complex. Elected officials must balance the demands of their constituents with the need to make informed decisions based on evidence and expert advice. Additionally, public opinion is not always uniform, and leaders must navigate competing interests and perspectives.

Public opinion can also be shaped by external factors, such as media coverage, political campaigns, and interest group advocacy. Understanding how these factors influence public opinion is essential for ensuring that democratic processes remain fair and transparent.

Safeguarding Democratic Institutions

Democratic institutions are the structures and processes that support the functioning of democracy. These include the legislative, executive, and judicial branches of government, as well as electoral systems, the free press, and civil society organizations. Safeguarding these institutions is essential for maintaining the health and stability of democratic societies.

Strengthening the Rule of Law

The rule of law is a fundamental principle of democracy, ensuring that all individuals and institutions are subject to the law and that laws are applied fairly and consistently. Strengthening the rule of law requires a commitment to the independence and integrity of the judiciary, the protection of individual rights, and the enforcement of legal standards.

Judicial independence is essential for maintaining the rule of law. Judges must be free from political pressure and influence to make impartial decisions based on the law. Safeguarding judicial independence involves measures to prevent the politicization of judicial appointments, ensure adequate funding for the judiciary, and protect judges from threats and intimidation.

The protection of individual rights is another key component of the rule of law. Democracies must ensure that laws are designed to protect the rights and freedoms of all citizens, including minority groups. This requires vigilance against discriminatory practices, abuses of power, and efforts to undermine civil liberties.

Ensuring Fair and Transparent Elections

Free and fair elections are a cornerstone of democracy, providing citizens with the opportunity to choose their representatives and hold them accountable. Ensuring the integrity of the electoral process requires measures to prevent fraud, protect voting rights, and promote transparency.

One of the primary challenges in ensuring fair elections is protecting the right to vote. Efforts to suppress voter turnout, such as restrictive voter ID laws, gerrymandering, and purging voter rolls, undermine the democratic process. Safeguarding voting rights involves removing barriers to participation, providing accessible voting options, and ensuring that all eligible citizens can exercise their right to vote.

Transparency in the electoral process is also essential. This includes measures to ensure that campaign financing is transparent, that voters have access to accurate information about candidates and issues, and that election results are reported accurately and promptly. Independent oversight bodies and international observers can play a role in monitoring elections and ensuring their integrity.

Promoting Civic Engagement

Civic engagement is critical for the health of democracy, as it ensures that citizens are actively involved in the political process and that their voices are heard. Promoting civic engagement requires efforts to educate and empower citizens, encourage participation, and build a sense of community and shared responsibility.

Education plays a vital role in promoting civic engagement. Schools and educational programs can provide students with the knowledge and skills needed to understand the political system, engage in informed discussions, and participate in civic activities. Civic education should emphasize the importance of democratic values, such as tolerance, respect for diversity, and the rule of law.

Efforts to encourage participation can include initiatives to increase voter turnout, support grassroots organizations, and create opportunities for citizens to engage in community service and advocacy. Building a culture of civic engagement involves fostering a sense of belonging and shared purpose, where individuals feel that their contributions can make a difference.

Protecting the Free Press

A free and independent press is essential for the functioning of democracy, as it provides citizens with the information they need to make informed decisions and hold government officials accountable. Protecting the free press involves safeguarding press freedom, ensuring access to information, and promoting ethical journalism.

Press freedom requires legal protections that prevent government censorship and interference in the media. This includes laws that protect journalists from harassment and intimidation, as well as measures to ensure that media organizations can operate independently and without undue pressure.

Access to information is another key component of a free press. Governments should ensure that information about public policies, decisions, and activities is readily available to the public. Transparency measures, such as freedom of information laws, can help to ensure that citizens have access to the information they need to hold their government accountable.

Promoting ethical journalism involves encouraging media organizations to adhere to standards of accuracy, fairness, and impartiality. This includes providing transparency about sources and methods, correcting errors promptly, and avoiding sensationalism and bias. Media organizations can also play a role in educating the public about media literacy and the importance of consuming information critically.

Chapter 5: Economic Policies Under Project 2025

Tax Reforms and Fiscal Policies

Economic policies under Project 2025 focus heavily on tax reforms and fiscal policies designed to stimulate growth, enhance efficiency, and ensure fiscal responsibility. These measures are rooted in conservative economic principles that prioritize limited government intervention, free-market dynamics, and the promotion of individual entrepreneurship and investment.

Tax Reforms

One of the cornerstone elements of Project 2025's economic agenda is comprehensive tax reform. Advocates argue that the current tax system is overly complex, burdensome, and hampers economic growth. The proposed reforms aim to simplify the tax code, reduce tax rates, and eliminate loopholes and deductions that favor specific groups or industries.

Simplification of the Tax Code

The simplification of the tax code is a central goal of Project 2025. The existing tax system is seen as convoluted, with myriad rules and regulations that create confusion and increase compliance costs for individuals and businesses. By simplifying the tax code, Project 2025 seeks to make it more transparent and easier to navigate.

Reduction of Tax Rates

Lowering tax rates is a key component of the proposed reforms. The idea is that reducing taxes on individuals and businesses will increase disposable income and capital available for investment, thereby stimulating economic activity. Specifically, Project 2025 advocates for lowering marginal income tax rates, reducing corporate tax rates, and simplifying capital gains taxes.

Elimination of Loopholes and Deductions

Eliminating loopholes and deductions is another significant aspect of the tax reform agenda. The current tax code contains numerous provisions that allow certain individuals and businesses to reduce their tax liability through various deductions and credits. Project 2025 aims to eliminate many of these loopholes to create a fairer and more equitable tax system, ensuring that everyone pays their fair share.

Introduction of a Flat Tax

Some proponents within Project 2025 advocate for the introduction of a flat tax, where a single tax rate is applied to all income levels. The flat tax model is seen as a way to further simplify the tax system, reduce administrative costs, and eliminate the progressive nature of the current tax structure. However, this proposal is controversial and faces significant opposition from those who argue that it disproportionately benefits higher-income individuals and could lead to increased income inequality.

Fiscal Policies

In addition to tax reforms, Project 2025 emphasizes fiscal policies aimed at reducing government spending, addressing the national debt, and promoting fiscal responsibility. These policies are driven by the belief that excessive government spending and debt pose significant risks to economic stability and growth.

Reducing Government Spending

A key priority of Project 2025 is to reduce government spending. Proponents argue that the federal government has grown too large and that its spending habits are unsustainable. They advocate for a comprehensive review of federal programs and agencies to identify areas where spending can be cut or streamlined. This includes reducing funding for programs deemed inefficient or unnecessary and implementing measures to improve the efficiency of government operations.

Balancing the Budget

Balancing the federal budget is another critical objective. Project 2025 aims to achieve this by implementing spending cuts and fiscal discipline measures. The goal is to ensure that government revenues match or exceed expenditures, thereby reducing the need for borrowing and helping to stabilize the national debt. Balancing the budget is seen as essential for maintaining investor confidence and ensuring long-term economic stability.

Addressing the National Debt

The national debt is a significant concern for proponents of Project 2025. The initiative advocates for policies to address the debt by reducing annual deficits and implementing long-term strategies for debt reduction. This includes entitlement reform, where programs such as Social Security, Medicare, and Medicaid are restructured to ensure their sustainability. By addressing the national debt, Project 2025 aims to reduce the fiscal burden on future generations and ensure the government's financial stability.

Economic Growth Strategies

Project 2025 outlines several strategies aimed at fostering economic growth. These strategies are based on the principles of free-market economics, emphasizing deregulation, innovation, and investment in key areas to drive growth and improve the overall economic environment.

Deregulation

Deregulation is a central strategy under Project 2025. Proponents argue that excessive regulation stifles innovation, increases costs for businesses, and hampers economic growth. By reducing the regulatory burden, Project 2025 aims to create a more favorable environment for businesses to thrive.

Reducing Regulatory Burdens

One of the primary goals is to reduce the number and complexity of regulations that businesses must comply with. This includes streamlining approval processes, eliminating redundant regulations, and ensuring that new regulations are based on sound economic analysis. The aim is to make it easier for businesses to operate, innovate, and expand.

Promoting Regulatory Transparency

Project 2025 also emphasizes the importance of regulatory transparency. Ensuring that regulations are clear, predictable, and consistently applied is seen as essential for fostering a stable and competitive business environment. By promoting transparency, Project 2025 seeks to reduce uncertainty and build confidence among investors and entrepreneurs.

Innovation and Technology

Innovation and technology are key drivers of economic growth. Project 2025 outlines several initiatives to promote innovation and leverage technology to enhance productivity and competitiveness.

Investment in Research and Development

Increasing investment in research and development (R&D) is a priority. Project 2025 advocates for policies that encourage both public and private investment in R&D, including tax incentives for businesses that invest in innovative technologies and support for research institutions. By fostering a culture of innovation, Project 2025 aims to position the United States as a global leader in technological advancements.

Supporting Emerging Technologies

Project 2025 also emphasizes the importance of supporting emerging technologies such as artificial intelligence, biotechnology, and renewable energy. Policies aimed at fostering the development and deployment of these technologies include funding for research, incentives for adoption, and collaboration between government, industry, and academia. By supporting emerging technologies, Project 2025 seeks to create new industries and job opportunities.

Infrastructure Investment

Infrastructure investment is another critical component of Project 2025's economic growth strategy. Modernizing and expanding the nation's infrastructure is seen as essential for enhancing productivity, reducing costs, and improving quality of life.

Modernizing Transportation Infrastructure

One of the key areas of focus is modernizing transportation infrastructure, including roads, bridges, railways, and airports. Project 2025 advocates for increased investment in these areas to improve efficiency, reduce congestion, and enhance safety. Modern transportation infrastructure is also seen as critical for supporting economic activity and facilitating trade.

Expanding Digital Infrastructure

Expanding digital infrastructure, such as broadband internet access, is another priority. Project 2025 aims to ensure that all Americans have access to high-speed internet, recognizing that digital connectivity is essential for economic participation and innovation. Policies include incentives for private investment in broadband infrastructure, as well as public funding for underserved areas.

Investing in Energy Infrastructure

Energy infrastructure is also a focus, with Project 2025 advocating for investment in a diverse and resilient energy grid. This includes supporting the development of renewable energy sources, such as solar and wind, as well as modernizing existing infrastructure to ensure reliability and efficiency. By investing in energy infrastructure, Project 2025 aims to support economic growth while promoting environmental sustainability.

Impact on Various Sectors

The economic policies under Project 2025 have significant implications for various sectors of the economy. By examining the potential impact on key industries, we can gain a better understanding of how these policies may shape the future economic landscape.

Manufacturing

The manufacturing sector stands to benefit significantly from the policies outlined in Project 2025. Deregulation, tax reforms, and infrastructure investment are expected to create a more favorable environment for manufacturers, leading to increased productivity and competitiveness.

Deregulation and Innovation

Reducing regulatory burdens will likely lower operational costs for manufacturers, enabling them to invest more in innovation and technology. This could lead to the development of new products and processes, enhancing the sector's overall efficiency and competitiveness.

Tax Incentives

Tax reforms, including lower corporate tax rates and incentives for capital investment, are expected to stimulate investment in manufacturing. By reducing the tax burden, Project 2025 aims to encourage manufacturers to expand their operations and create new jobs.

Infrastructure Improvements

Investment in transportation and digital infrastructure will also benefit the manufacturing sector by improving supply chain efficiency and reducing logistics costs. Modern infrastructure is essential for supporting manufacturing operations and facilitating trade.

Energy

The energy sector is another area where Project 2025's policies are expected to have a significant impact. By promoting energy independence and supporting the development of diverse energy sources, the initiative aims to create a more resilient and sustainable energy landscape.

Support for Renewable Energy

Project 2025 emphasizes the importance of supporting renewable energy sources such as solar, wind, and hydroelectric power. Policies aimed at encouraging investment in these technologies include tax incentives, grants, and research funding. By promoting renewable energy, Project 2025 seeks to reduce dependence on fossil fuels and enhance environmental sustainability.

Modernizing the Energy Grid

Investment in modernizing the energy grid is also a priority. Upgrading the grid to accommodate new energy sources and improve efficiency is seen as essential for ensuring a reliable and resilient energy supply. This includes investments in smart grid technologies, energy storage solutions, and cybersecurity measures.

Energy Independence

Promoting energy independence is another key goal. Project 2025 advocates for policies that support domestic energy production, including oil, natural gas, and nuclear energy. By reducing reliance on foreign energy sources, Project 2025 aims to enhance national security and stabilize energy prices.

Technology and Innovation

The technology sector is poised to thrive under the policies outlined in Project 2025. By fostering a culture of innovation and supporting the development of emerging technologies, the initiative aims to position the United States as a global leader in technology.

Investment in R&D

Increased investment in research and development is expected to drive innovation in the technology sector. Tax incentives for R&D, funding for research institutions, and support for public-private partnerships will likely lead to the development of new technologies and products.

Support for Emerging Technologies

Project 2025 emphasizes the importance of supporting emerging technologies such as artificial intelligence, biotechnology, and quantum computing. Policies aimed at fostering the development and deployment of these technologies include funding for research, incentives for adoption, and collaboration between government, industry, and academia.

Digital Infrastructure

Expanding digital infrastructure, such as broadband internet access, will benefit the technology sector by enhancing connectivity and enabling the growth of digital services. Ensuring that all Americans have access to high-speed internet is essential for supporting innovation and economic participation.

Healthcare

The healthcare sector is expected to undergo significant changes under Project 2025's policies. By promoting market-based solutions and increasing competition, the initiative aims to reduce costs and improve access to quality care.

Market-Based Solutions

Project 2025 advocates for market-based solutions to address the challenges facing the healthcare system. This includes promoting competition among insurers, providing tax credits for individuals to purchase insurance, and allowing for the sale of insurance across state lines. By increasing competition, Project 2025 aims to lower healthcare costs and improve quality.

Reforming Entitlement Programs

Reforming entitlement programs such as Medicare and Medicaid is another priority. Project 2025 proposes shifting toward premium support for Medicare, where beneficiaries receive a fixed amount to purchase insurance, and block grants for Medicaid, giving states more flexibility to design their programs. These reforms are intended to reduce costs and improve efficiency.

Investment in Healthcare Technology

Increasing investment in healthcare technology is also emphasized. Project 2025 advocates for policies that support the development and adoption of technologies such as telemedicine, electronic health records, and personalized medicine. By leveraging technology, the initiative aims to improve access to care and enhance patient outcomes.

Chapter 6: Social Policies and Their Impact

Education and Healthcare Reforms

Project 2025 emphasizes comprehensive reforms in both education and healthcare, recognizing their critical roles in shaping the well-being and future of American society. These reforms aim to address inefficiencies, improve access, and ensure that systems are better aligned with the needs and values of the populace.

Education Reforms

Education is seen as the foundation of a prosperous and informed society. Project 2025 outlines several key reforms designed to improve the quality of education, enhance student outcomes, and promote choice and accountability within the education system.

School Choice and Vouchers

One of the primary proposals under Project 2025 is the expansion of school choice programs. This includes the implementation of vouchers, which allow parents to use public funding to enroll their children in private schools, charter schools, or other alternative educational institutions. The rationale behind this proposal is to foster competition among schools, which proponents believe will drive improvements in quality and innovation.

Charter Schools and Education Savings Accounts

Charter schools are also a significant focus. These publicly funded but independently operated schools offer greater flexibility in terms of curriculum and management, allowing for more innovative approaches to education. Additionally, Education Savings Accounts (ESAs) are proposed, which enable parents to allocate funds for various educational expenses, including tuition, tutoring, and online courses, thereby increasing personalized learning opportunities.

Accountability and Standards

Improving accountability and standards is another critical aspect of the education reforms. Project 2025 advocates for rigorous assessment systems to evaluate student performance, teacher effectiveness, and school quality. By implementing standardized testing and performance-based evaluations, the initiative aims to ensure that all students receive a high-quality education and that schools are held accountable for their outcomes.

Teacher Performance and Incentives

Teacher performance is crucial to student success. Project 2025 proposes performance-based pay and professional development programs to incentivize and support teachers. By rewarding high-performing teachers and providing opportunities for continuous improvement, the initiative seeks to attract and retain talented educators.

Curriculum and STEM Emphasis

Reforming the curriculum to emphasize Science, Technology, Engineering, and Mathematics (STEM) education is another key priority. Project 2025 aims to prepare students for the demands of the modern workforce by enhancing STEM programs and integrating technology into the classroom. This approach is intended to foster critical thinking, problem-solving skills, and innovation.

Healthcare Reforms

Healthcare reform under Project 2025 focuses on increasing access, reducing costs, and improving the overall quality of care. The initiative proposes market-based solutions to address the inefficiencies and challenges facing the current healthcare system.

Market-Based Solutions

Project 2025 advocates for increasing competition within the healthcare market. This includes allowing insurance companies to sell policies across state lines, thereby expanding choices for consumers and driving down costs through competition. The initiative also proposes tax credits to help individuals purchase health insurance, making it more affordable for those without employer-sponsored coverage.

Repeal and Replace the Affordable Care Act

A central aspect of the healthcare reforms is the repeal and replacement of the Affordable Care Act (ACA). Project 2025 argues that the ACA has led to higher premiums and reduced choices for consumers. The proposed replacement would focus on market-based approaches, emphasizing individual responsibility and consumer choice. This includes high-deductible health plans paired with Health Savings Accounts (HSAs), which encourage individuals to save for medical expenses and make informed healthcare decisions.

Medicare and Medicaid Reforms

Reforming Medicare and Medicaid is another critical component of the healthcare agenda. Project 2025 proposes transitioning Medicare to a premium support system, where beneficiaries receive a fixed amount to purchase insurance on the private market. This approach is intended to increase competition and control costs. For Medicaid, the initiative advocates for block grants, giving states greater flexibility to design and manage their programs according to their specific needs.

Telemedicine and Healthcare Technology

Embracing telemedicine and healthcare technology is also emphasized. Project 2025 supports policies that promote the use of telehealth services, electronic health records, and other technological advancements to improve access and efficiency. By leveraging technology, the initiative aims to enhance patient care, reduce costs, and expand access to underserved populations.

Prescription Drug Costs

Addressing the high cost of prescription drugs is another priority. Project 2025 proposes measures to increase transparency in drug pricing, promote the use of generic medications, and encourage competition within the pharmaceutical industry. By implementing these reforms, the initiative aims to make prescription medications more affordable for consumers.

Social Justice and Equality Issues

Social justice and equality are central to the conservative vision of a fair and just society. Project 2025 outlines several policies aimed at addressing issues of social justice and promoting equality across various dimensions, including race, gender, and economic status.

Criminal Justice Reform

Reforming the criminal justice system is a key component of the social justice agenda. Project 2025 advocates for policies that promote fairness, reduce recidivism, and ensure public safety.

Sentencing Reform

One of the primary areas of focus is sentencing reform. Project 2025 proposes reducing mandatory minimum sentences for non-violent offenses and expanding alternatives to incarceration, such as drug treatment programs and community service. The goal is to address the root causes of crime and provide individuals with opportunities for rehabilitation.

Police Accountability and Training

Improving police accountability and training is another critical aspect. Project 2025 supports policies that enhance transparency in law enforcement, including the use of body cameras and independent oversight of police conduct. Additionally, the initiative emphasizes the importance of comprehensive training for officers, focusing on de-escalation techniques, cultural competency, and mental health awareness.

Reentry Programs

Supporting reentry programs for formerly incarcerated individuals is also a priority. Project 2025 advocates for initiatives that provide education, job training, and housing assistance to help individuals reintegrate into society and reduce recidivism rates.

Economic Equality

Addressing economic inequality is essential for promoting social justice. Project 2025 outlines several policies aimed at expanding economic opportunities and ensuring that all individuals have the chance to succeed.

Workforce Development

Investing in workforce development is a key strategy. Project 2025 proposes expanding vocational training and apprenticeship programs to equip individuals with the skills needed for high-demand jobs. By providing targeted training and education, the initiative aims to bridge the skills gap and enhance economic mobility.

Entrepreneurship and Small Business Support

Supporting entrepreneurship and small businesses is another critical component. Project 2025 advocates for policies that reduce regulatory burdens, provide access to capital, and offer mentorship and support programs for aspiring entrepreneurs. By fostering a culture of entrepreneurship, the initiative seeks to create jobs and drive economic growth.

Affordable Housing

Ensuring access to affordable housing is also emphasized. Project 2025 supports measures to increase the supply of affordable housing, including incentives for developers, zoning reforms, and the expansion of housing assistance programs. By addressing the housing affordability crisis, the initiative aims to provide stability and security for individuals and families.

Gender Equality

Promoting gender equality is an integral part of the social justice agenda. Project 2025 outlines several policies aimed at addressing gender disparities and ensuring equal opportunities for all.

Equal Pay

One of the primary goals is to address the gender pay gap. Project 2025 advocates for policies that promote pay transparency and ensure that women receive equal pay for equal work. This includes measures to prevent wage discrimination and support for workplace policies that promote gender equity.

Family Support Policies

Supporting family-friendly policies is another critical aspect. Project 2025 proposes initiatives such as paid family leave, affordable childcare, and flexible work arrangements to help working parents balance their professional and personal responsibilities. By providing support for families, the initiative aims to promote gender equality in the workplace and at home.

Women in Leadership

Encouraging women to pursue leadership roles is also emphasized. Project 2025 supports programs that provide mentorship, networking opportunities, and leadership training for women. By promoting gender diversity in leadership, the initiative seeks to create a more inclusive and equitable society.

The Future of Social Security and Welfare

Social Security and welfare programs are essential components of the social safety net, providing support for vulnerable populations and ensuring economic security. Project 2025 outlines several reforms aimed at ensuring the sustainability and effectiveness of these programs.

Social Security Reform

Reforming Social Security is a key priority. Project 2025 advocates for measures to ensure the long-term solvency of the program while maintaining benefits for current and future retirees.

Gradual Increase in Retirement Age

One of the proposed reforms is a gradual increase in the retirement age. As life expectancy continues to rise, adjusting the retirement age is seen as a way to ensure the sustainability of Social Security. Project 2025 proposes increasing the retirement age incrementally over time, allowing individuals to plan for their retirement accordingly.

Means Testing for Benefits

Introducing means testing for Social Security benefits is another proposal. Under this approach, benefits would be adjusted based on an individual's income and assets, ensuring that those with greater financial resources receive reduced benefits. This is intended to focus resources on those who need them most and reduce the overall cost of the program.

Personal Retirement Accounts

Project 2025 also advocates for the introduction of personal retirement accounts. These accounts would allow individuals to invest a portion of their Social Security contributions in private investment options. By giving individuals more control over their retirement savings, the initiative aims to enhance retirement security and provide opportunities for greater returns.

Welfare Reform

Reforming welfare programs is another critical aspect of Project 2025's social policy agenda. The initiative emphasizes the importance of promoting self-sufficiency and reducing dependency on government assistance.

Work Requirements

One of the key proposals is the implementation of work requirements for welfare recipients. Project 2025 advocates for policies that require able-bodied adults to participate in work or work-related activities, such as job training or community service, as a condition for receiving benefits. The goal is to encourage self-sufficiency and reduce long-term dependency on welfare programs.

Streamlining Programs

Streamlining and consolidating welfare programs is also emphasized. Project 2025 proposes reducing the complexity and redundancy of existing programs by consolidating them into a more cohesive and efficient system. This includes improving coordination between federal, state, and local agencies to ensure that resources are used effectively and that individuals receive the support they need.

Incentives for Employment

Providing incentives for employment is another critical aspect. Project 2025 supports policies that offer financial incentives, such as tax credits and wage subsidies, to encourage individuals to enter and remain in the workforce. By promoting employment, the initiative aims to enhance economic mobility and reduce poverty.

Education and Training Programs

Investing in education and training programs for welfare recipients is also a priority. Project 2025 advocates for initiatives that provide access to education, job training, and skills development to help individuals transition from welfare to work. By equipping individuals with the skills needed to succeed in the labor market, the initiative aims to promote self-sufficiency and economic independence.

Chapter 7: Foreign Policy and National Security

Project 2025's Global Vision

Project 2025's approach to foreign policy and national security is underpinned by a commitment to maintaining American leadership on the global stage while safeguarding national interests. The initiative envisions a world where the United States leverages its economic, military, and diplomatic strengths to promote stability, prosperity, and democratic values.

Upholding American Leadership

One of the primary objectives of Project 2025 is to uphold and reinforce American leadership globally. This involves asserting U.S. influence in key regions, ensuring that America remains a dominant player in international affairs, and countering the influence of rival powers such as China and Russia.

Economic Influence

Economic strength is a cornerstone of American global leadership. Project 2025 emphasizes the importance of a robust economy in supporting foreign policy objectives. By maintaining a competitive economy and fostering international trade, the United States can exert considerable influence over global economic policies and practices. Trade agreements, economic sanctions, and foreign aid are viewed as vital tools for promoting American interests and values abroad.

Military Dominance

Military strength is another critical component of American leadership. Project 2025 advocates for maintaining and enhancing the U.S. military's capabilities to ensure that it can respond effectively to a wide range of threats. This includes investing in advanced technologies, modernizing existing equipment, and ensuring the readiness and capability of the armed forces.

Diplomatic Engagement

Diplomatic engagement is essential for advancing American interests and promoting stability. Project 2025 emphasizes the importance of active participation in international organizations, such as the United Nations, NATO, and regional alliances. By engaging diplomatically, the United States can shape international norms, build coalitions, and address global challenges collaboratively.

Promoting Democratic Values

Promoting democratic values is a central tenet of Project 2025's global vision. The initiative views the spread of democracy as essential for creating a more stable and just world. This involves supporting democratic movements, providing assistance to emerging democracies, and advocating for human rights and the rule of law.

Support for Democratic Movements

Project 2025 proposes increasing support for democratic movements around the world. This includes providing financial assistance, technical support, and diplomatic backing to groups advocating for democratic reforms. By supporting these movements, the United States can help foster more democratic and accountable governments.

Human Rights Advocacy

Human rights advocacy is another key focus. Project 2025 emphasizes the importance of promoting and protecting human rights globally. This involves speaking out against abuses, imposing sanctions on regimes that violate human rights, and supporting international efforts to hold violators accountable. By championing human rights, the United States can help create a more just and equitable world.

Rule of Law

Promoting the rule of law is also emphasized. Project 2025 advocates for initiatives that strengthen legal institutions and promote good governance. This includes providing support for judicial reforms, anti-corruption measures, and the development of legal frameworks that protect individual rights. By promoting the rule of law, the United States can help build more stable and resilient societies.

Defense Strategies and Military Readiness

Maintaining a strong and capable military is essential for ensuring national security and protecting American interests. Project 2025 outlines several defense strategies aimed at enhancing military readiness, modernizing capabilities, and addressing emerging threats.

Enhancing Military Readiness

Military readiness is a top priority under Project 2025. Ensuring that the armed forces are prepared to respond to a wide range of threats is seen as essential for maintaining national security.

Training and Recruitment

Improving training and recruitment is a key focus. Project 2025 advocates for policies that attract and retain top talent within the military. This includes competitive compensation packages, education benefits, and career development opportunities. Additionally, the initiative emphasizes the importance of rigorous training programs that prepare service members for the complexities of modern warfare.

Operational Readiness

Enhancing operational readiness is also emphasized. Project 2025 proposes increasing funding for maintenance and logistics to ensure that military equipment is in optimal condition. This includes investing in supply chain resilience, ensuring adequate stockpiles of critical materials, and enhancing the military's ability to deploy rapidly and effectively.

Joint Operations

Promoting joint operations is another priority. Project 2025 advocates for greater integration and coordination among the different branches of the armed forces. By enhancing interoperability and fostering a culture of collaboration, the military can operate more effectively across different domains and respond to complex threats.

Modernizing Capabilities

Modernizing military capabilities is essential for maintaining technological superiority and addressing emerging threats. Project 2025 outlines several initiatives aimed at enhancing the military's technological edge.

Advanced Technologies

Investing in advanced technologies is a critical component of modernization. Project 2025 advocates for increased funding for research and development in areas such as artificial intelligence, cyber capabilities, and unmanned systems. By leveraging these technologies, the military can enhance its operational effectiveness and maintain a competitive edge.

Cybersecurity

Enhancing cybersecurity is another key focus. Project 2025 emphasizes the importance of protecting critical infrastructure and military systems from cyber threats. This includes investing in cyber defense capabilities, enhancing information sharing and collaboration with allies, and developing strategies to deter and respond to cyberattacks.

Space Capabilities

Expanding space capabilities is also prioritized. Project 2025 advocates for the development of space-based assets to enhance communication, surveillance, and navigation. This includes investments in satellite technology, space-based sensors, and the development of policies to protect space assets from potential adversaries.

Addressing Emerging Threats

The security landscape is constantly evolving, with new and emerging threats posing significant challenges. Project 2025 outlines several strategies to address these threats and ensure national security.

Terrorism and Asymmetric Warfare

Combating terrorism and asymmetric warfare remains a top priority. Project 2025 advocates for a comprehensive approach that includes intelligence gathering, counterterrorism operations, and efforts to address the root causes of extremism. This includes partnerships with other nations, support for counterterrorism initiatives, and measures to disrupt terrorist financing and logistics.

Great Power Competition

Addressing the challenge posed by great power competition, particularly with China and Russia, is another critical focus. Project 2025 emphasizes the importance of maintaining a robust deterrent capability and developing strategies to counter the influence of these rival powers. This includes enhancing military presence in key regions, building alliances, and investing in capabilities that counter the specific threats posed by these nations.

Biological and Chemical Threats

Preparing for biological and chemical threats is also emphasized. Project 2025 advocates for measures to enhance the military's ability to respond to biological and chemical attacks. This includes investments in detection and response capabilities, medical countermeasures, and training programs for service members.

Diplomatic Relations and International Alliances

Strong diplomatic relations and international alliances are essential for advancing American interests and promoting global stability. Project 2025 outlines several strategies aimed at enhancing diplomatic engagement, building alliances, and addressing global challenges collaboratively.

Strengthening Diplomatic Engagement

Active and effective diplomatic engagement is crucial for advancing American interests and promoting stability. Project 2025 emphasizes the importance of a robust and proactive diplomatic strategy.

Diplomatic Presence

Increasing the U.S. diplomatic presence worldwide is a key priority. Project 2025 advocates for the expansion of diplomatic missions and the deployment of skilled diplomats to key regions. This includes opening new embassies and consulates, enhancing the capacity of existing missions, and ensuring that diplomats have the resources and support needed to perform their duties effectively.

Bilateral and Multilateral Engagement

Project 2025 emphasizes the importance of both bilateral and multilateral engagement. This includes strengthening relationships with key allies and partners through bilateral agreements and initiatives. Additionally, the initiative advocates for active participation in multilateral organizations, such as the United Nations, NATO, and regional alliances, to address global challenges collaboratively.

Public Diplomacy

Enhancing public diplomacy is also prioritized. Project 2025 advocates for initiatives that promote American values and culture abroad. This includes cultural exchange programs, educational initiatives, and efforts to counter misinformation and promote a positive image of the United States globally.

Building and Maintaining Alliances

Strong alliances are essential for promoting global stability and addressing shared challenges. Project 2025 outlines several strategies aimed at building and maintaining alliances with key partners.

NATO and Transatlantic Relations

Strengthening NATO and transatlantic relations is a critical focus. Project 2025 advocates for increased investment in NATO, enhanced cooperation with European allies, and efforts to address common security challenges. This includes initiatives to improve interoperability, share intelligence, and conduct joint military exercises.

Asia-Pacific Alliances

Building and maintaining alliances in the Asia-Pacific region is also emphasized. Project 2025 advocates for strengthening relationships with key allies such as Japan, South Korea, and Australia. This includes enhancing military cooperation, expanding economic ties, and working together to address regional security challenges, particularly the threat posed by North Korea and the rise of China.

Middle East Partnerships

Maintaining partnerships in the Middle East is another priority. Project 2025 supports continued engagement with key allies such as Israel, Saudi Arabia, and other Gulf states. This includes efforts to address regional conflicts, counter terrorism, and promote stability. Additionally, the initiative advocates for supporting peace initiatives and efforts to resolve longstanding conflicts in the region.

Africa and Latin America

Expanding engagement with Africa and Latin America is also emphasized. Project 2025 advocates for increased diplomatic, economic, and security cooperation with nations in these regions. This includes initiatives to promote economic development, enhance security cooperation, and support democratic governance.

Addressing Global Challenges

Project 2025 outlines several strategies aimed at addressing global challenges collaboratively. These challenges include climate change, global health, and international security.

Climate Change

Addressing climate change is a key focus. Project 2025 advocates for international cooperation to reduce greenhouse gas emissions, promote renewable energy, and enhance resilience to climate impacts. This includes participation in international agreements, support for climate-related research, and efforts to promote sustainable development.

Global Health

Enhancing global health is also prioritized. Project 2025 supports initiatives to address global health challenges such as infectious diseases, pandemics, and access to healthcare. This includes funding for international health organizations, support for disease prevention and treatment programs, and efforts to improve healthcare infrastructure in developing countries.

International Security

Promoting international security is another critical focus. Project 2025 advocates for measures to address global security challenges, including nuclear proliferation, terrorism, and transnational crime. This includes efforts to strengthen international security frameworks, enhance cooperation with allies, and support initiatives to promote peace and stability.

Chapter 8: Environmental and Energy Policies

Approaches to Climate Change

Climate change represents one of the most pressing challenges of our time, with far-reaching impacts on the environment, economy, and society. Project 2025 outlines a comprehensive approach to addressing climate change that includes mitigation, adaptation, and resilience strategies.

Mitigation Strategies

Mitigation efforts are focused on reducing greenhouse gas emissions to slow the pace of climate change. Project 2025 emphasizes several key strategies for achieving significant emissions reductions.

Transition to Renewable Energy

One of the primary mitigation strategies is transitioning to renewable energy sources such as solar, wind, and hydroelectric power. Project 2025 advocates for policies that incentivize the development and deployment of renewable energy technologies. This includes tax credits for renewable energy projects, funding for research and development, and support for grid modernization to accommodate variable renewable energy sources.

Energy Efficiency

Improving energy efficiency is another critical component of the mitigation strategy. Project 2025 proposes initiatives to enhance energy efficiency in buildings, transportation, and industry. This includes implementing stricter energy efficiency standards, providing incentives for energy-efficient upgrades, and promoting the adoption of energy-saving technologies.

Carbon Pricing

Project 2025 also explores the potential of carbon pricing mechanisms, such as carbon taxes or cap-and-trade systems, to reduce emissions. By putting a price on carbon, these mechanisms create economic incentives for businesses and individuals to reduce their carbon footprint. The revenue generated from carbon pricing can be used to fund climate mitigation and adaptation projects, further accelerating the transition to a low-carbon economy.

Reforestation and Land Use

Reforestation and improved land use practices are additional strategies for mitigating climate change. Project 2025 supports initiatives to restore forests, protect natural habitats, and promote sustainable agriculture. These efforts not only sequester carbon but also enhance biodiversity and improve ecosystem services.

Adaptation and Resilience

In addition to mitigation, Project 2025 emphasizes the importance of adaptation and resilience to cope with the impacts of climate change that are already occurring.

Infrastructure Resilience

Enhancing the resilience of infrastructure is a key focus. Project 2025 advocates for investments in resilient infrastructure that can withstand extreme weather events and other climate-related impacts. This includes upgrading transportation systems, reinforcing coastal defenses, and ensuring that critical infrastructure such as power grids and water supply systems are resilient to climate risks.

Disaster Preparedness and Response

Improving disaster preparedness and response capabilities is also emphasized. Project 2025 supports initiatives to enhance early warning systems, develop comprehensive disaster response plans, and provide resources for emergency management agencies. By improving preparedness, the initiative aims to reduce the human and economic costs of climate-related disasters.

Community-Based Adaptation

Project 2025 recognizes the importance of community-based adaptation strategies. This involves working with local communities to develop and implement adaptation plans that address specific vulnerabilities and build local capacity to respond to climate impacts. Community engagement and participation are seen as essential for ensuring that adaptation efforts are effective and equitable.

Public Health and Climate Change

Addressing the public health impacts of climate change is another priority. Project 2025 advocates for measures to protect public health, such as monitoring and addressing climate-related health risks, improving healthcare infrastructure, and promoting public awareness of health issues related to climate change.

Energy Independence and Sustainability

Achieving energy independence and sustainability is a central goal of Project 2025's environmental and energy policies. This involves reducing dependence on foreign energy sources, promoting sustainable energy production, and ensuring that energy systems are resilient and secure.

Energy Independence

Energy independence is essential for national security and economic stability. Project 2025 outlines several strategies to reduce dependence on foreign energy and enhance domestic energy production.

Domestic Energy Production

Increasing domestic energy production is a key priority. Project 2025 supports the development of diverse energy sources, including renewable energy, natural gas, and nuclear power. By promoting a diverse energy mix, the initiative aims to reduce reliance on imported energy and enhance energy security.

Energy Infrastructure

Investing in energy infrastructure is also emphasized. Project 2025 advocates for the modernization of energy infrastructure, including the construction of pipelines, transmission lines, and storage facilities. This includes upgrading the electric grid to accommodate new energy sources and improve reliability.

Strategic Petroleum Reserve

Maintaining and enhancing the Strategic Petroleum Reserve (SPR) is another important aspect of energy independence. Project 2025 supports policies to ensure that the SPR is adequately funded and maintained to provide a buffer against potential disruptions in energy supply.

Sustainable Energy Production

Promoting sustainable energy production is essential for ensuring long-term energy security and environmental protection. Project 2025 outlines several initiatives to promote sustainability in energy production.

Renewable Energy Development

As mentioned earlier, expanding renewable energy development is a central strategy. Project 2025 supports policies that encourage the growth of solar, wind, hydroelectric, and geothermal energy. This includes providing incentives for renewable energy projects, streamlining permitting processes, and investing in research and development.

Nuclear Energy

Nuclear energy is recognized as a key component of a sustainable energy future. Project 2025 advocates for the expansion of nuclear energy, including the development of advanced nuclear reactors and small modular reactors (SMRs). Nuclear energy is seen as a reliable and low-carbon energy source that can provide baseload power and complement renewable energy sources.

Natural Gas

Natural gas is also seen as a transitional fuel that can help reduce carbon emissions while renewable energy capacity is scaled up. Project 2025 supports the development of natural gas infrastructure, including pipelines and export facilities, to ensure a stable and secure supply of natural gas.

Bioenergy and Biofuels

Promoting bioenergy and biofuels is another aspect of sustainable energy production. Project 2025 advocates for the development of bioenergy technologies that convert biomass into electricity, heat, and transportation fuels. This includes supporting research and development, providing incentives for bioenergy projects, and promoting the use of biofuels in transportation.

Balancing Economic Growth with Environmental Protection

Balancing economic growth with environmental protection is a central challenge for policymakers. Project 2025 outlines several strategies to achieve this balance, recognizing that sustainable economic growth and environmental protection are not mutually exclusive but can be mutually reinforcing.

Green Economy

Promoting the development of a green economy is a key strategy for balancing economic growth with environmental protection. A green economy is one that generates growth and employment while reducing environmental impacts and promoting sustainability.

Green Jobs

Project 2025 advocates for the creation of green jobs in sectors such as renewable energy, energy efficiency, and environmental conservation. This includes providing training and education programs to equip workers with the skills needed for green jobs, as well as incentives for businesses that create green employment opportunities.

Sustainable Businesses

Supporting the growth of sustainable businesses is also emphasized. Project 2025 supports policies that encourage businesses to adopt sustainable practices, such as reducing waste, conserving energy, and sourcing materials responsibly. This includes providing incentives for sustainable business practices and supporting the development of green technologies.

Circular Economy

Promoting a circular economy is another aspect of the green economy strategy. A circular economy is one in which resources are used more efficiently, waste is minimized, and materials are reused and recycled. Project 2025 advocates for policies that promote circular economy principles, such as extended producer responsibility, product design for longevity, and recycling infrastructure.

Environmental Regulations

Environmental regulations play a critical role in protecting natural resources and ensuring environmental sustainability. Project 2025 outlines a balanced approach to environmental regulation that protects the environment while supporting economic growth.

Smart Regulation

Project 2025 advocates for smart regulation that is based on sound science, cost-benefit analysis, and stakeholder engagement. Smart regulation aims to achieve environmental objectives in the most efficient and effective way possible, minimizing unnecessary burdens on businesses and consumers.

Regulatory Reform

Regulatory reform is another key focus. Project 2025 supports efforts to streamline and modernize environmental regulations, reducing complexity and improving clarity. This includes eliminating outdated or redundant regulations and ensuring that new regulations are designed to achieve their objectives without imposing unnecessary costs.

Market-Based Approaches

Project 2025 also supports market-based approaches to environmental protection, such as emissions trading and carbon pricing. Market-based approaches create economic incentives for businesses and individuals to reduce their environmental impact, promoting innovation and efficiency.

Conservation and Biodiversity

Protecting natural resources and biodiversity is essential for ensuring environmental sustainability. Project 2025 outlines several initiatives to promote conservation and protect ecosystems.

Protected Areas

Expanding and managing protected areas is a key strategy. Project 2025 advocates for the designation and management of national parks, wildlife refuges, and marine protected areas to conserve biodiversity and protect critical habitats. This includes providing funding for the management and restoration of protected areas and promoting sustainable tourism.

Habitat Restoration

Habitat restoration is also emphasized. Project 2025 supports initiatives to restore degraded ecosystems, such as wetlands, forests, and coastal areas. This includes funding for restoration projects, promoting best practices, and engaging local communities in restoration efforts.

Sustainable Agriculture and Forestry

Promoting sustainable agriculture and forestry is another priority. Project 2025 advocates for practices that conserve soil, water, and biodiversity, such as agroforestry, organic farming, and sustainable forest management. This includes providing incentives for sustainable practices and supporting research and development in sustainable agriculture and forestry.

Chapter 9: The Public Response

Reactions from Different Political Spectrums

Project 2025, with its comprehensive vision for the future of American governance, has elicited a wide range of reactions from across the political spectrum. Understanding these reactions is crucial for comprehending the broader implications of the initiative and the challenges it may face in implementation.

Conservative Support and Advocacy

The conservative base has largely embraced Project 2025, viewing it as a necessary and ambitious blueprint for restoring what they perceive as fundamental American values and principles. Supporters argue that the initiative addresses key concerns about the direction of the country and offers practical solutions to current challenges.

Economic Policy Enthusiasm

Conservatives particularly applaud the economic policies outlined in Project 2025, such as tax reforms, deregulation, and fiscal responsibility. These policies resonate with traditional conservative values of limited government, free enterprise, and individual responsibility. Supporters believe that these measures will spur economic growth, create jobs, and increase overall prosperity.

National Security and Defense

The focus on enhancing national security and military readiness also garners significant support from conservatives. The emphasis on maintaining a strong military, modernizing defense capabilities, and addressing emerging threats aligns with the conservative view that national defense is a paramount government responsibility. Supporters argue that these policies will ensure that the United States remains safe and secure in an increasingly volatile world.

Cultural and Social Values

Project 2025's commitment to preserving traditional cultural and social values is another aspect that appeals to the conservative base. Policies that protect religious freedom, promote family values, and oppose progressive social changes are seen as essential for maintaining the moral and cultural fabric of the nation. Conservative supporters believe that these policies will help restore a sense of stability and continuity in American society.

Liberal Criticism and Opposition

On the other end of the spectrum, liberals have expressed significant criticism and opposition to Project 2025. They argue that the initiative represents a regressive shift that threatens to undermine progress on social, economic, and environmental fronts.

Concerns About Social Inequality

One of the primary criticisms from liberals is that Project 2025's economic policies will exacerbate social inequality. They argue that tax cuts and deregulation disproportionately benefit the wealthy and large corporations, while doing little to address the needs of low- and middle-income Americans. Critics contend that these policies will widen the gap between rich and poor, leading to greater economic disparity and social instability.

Environmental and Climate Policy Criticism

Environmental policies under Project 2025 have also faced significant scrutiny. Liberals argue that the emphasis on energy independence through increased domestic production of fossil fuels and the promotion of nuclear energy overlooks the urgent need to address climate change. They contend that the initiative does not go far enough in promoting renewable energy and reducing greenhouse gas emissions, potentially jeopardizing the planet's future.

Civil Rights and Social Justice Concerns

Liberals are also concerned about the social and cultural policies outlined in Project 2025. They argue that policies aimed at preserving traditional values and limiting progressive social changes threaten to roll back gains made in civil rights, gender equality, and LGBTQ+ rights. Critics contend that these policies could marginalize vulnerable communities and undermine efforts to promote social justice and equality.

Centrist and Independent Perspectives

Reactions from centrists and independent voters are more mixed, reflecting a blend of support and skepticism. These individuals often weigh the potential benefits and drawbacks of Project 2025's policies on a case-by-case basis, without adhering strictly to ideological lines.

Support for Pragmatic Solutions

Many centrists and independents appreciate the pragmatic aspects of Project 2025, particularly in areas like economic policy and national security. They support efforts to streamline regulations, reduce government spending, and enhance military capabilities, viewing these measures as necessary for maintaining stability and promoting growth.

Concerns About Extremism

However, there is also concern among centrists and independents about the potential for extremism in some of Project 2025's proposals. They worry that an overly aggressive approach to deregulation and tax cuts could lead to negative economic consequences, while rigid social policies might alienate significant portions of the population. These voters often advocate for a more balanced approach that incorporates elements from both conservative and liberal perspectives.

Public Opinion and Grassroots Movements

Public opinion and grassroots movements play a crucial role in shaping the discourse around Project 2025. Understanding how these dynamics influence the initiative is essential for grasping its broader implications and potential for success.

Public Opinion Dynamics

Public opinion on Project 2025 is shaped by a variety of factors, including media coverage, political messaging, and personal experiences. These influences contribute to a complex and evolving landscape of public sentiment.

Media Influence

Media coverage plays a significant role in shaping public opinion on Project 2025. Different media outlets present varying perspectives on the initiative, often reflecting their ideological leanings. Conservative media generally portray Project 2025 in a positive light, emphasizing its potential benefits and aligning it with broader conservative values. In contrast, liberal media tend to highlight the potential drawbacks and criticisms, focusing on the risks and negative implications.

Political Messaging

Political messaging from key stakeholders also influences public opinion. Supporters of Project 2025, including conservative politicians and advocacy groups, use various platforms to promote the initiative and garner support. They emphasize the benefits of the proposed policies, such as economic growth, national security, and the preservation of traditional values. Opponents, including liberal politicians and activist organizations, counter these messages by highlighting the potential harms and advocating for alternative approaches.

Personal Experiences and Beliefs

Individual experiences and beliefs significantly shape public opinion. People's views on Project 2025 are often influenced by their personal economic situation, social values, and experiences with government policies. For example, individuals who have benefited from deregulation and tax cuts may be more supportive of the initiative, while those who have faced challenges due to reduced social services may be more critical.

Grassroots Movements

Grassroots movements are a powerful force in shaping public discourse and influencing policy decisions. These movements mobilize individuals and communities around shared concerns and goals, often playing a pivotal role in advocating for or against specific policies.

Supportive Movements

Several grassroots movements support Project 2025, driven by conservative and libertarian values. These movements advocate for limited government, economic freedom, and the protection of traditional values. Key supportive movements include:

Tea Party Movement

The Tea Party movement, which emerged in the late 2000s, remains a significant force in advocating for limited government and fiscal conservatism. Supporters of the Tea Party are likely to back Project 2025's proposals for tax cuts, deregulation, and reduced government spending.

Religious and Family Values Groups

Religious and family values groups are also strong supporters of Project 2025, particularly regarding its social and cultural policies. Organizations such as the Family Research Council and Focus on the Family advocate for policies that protect religious freedom, promote family values, and oppose progressive social changes.

Business and Industry Groups

Business and industry groups, including the Chamber of Commerce and various trade associations, support Project 2025's economic policies. These groups advocate for deregulation, tax cuts, and policies that promote economic growth and competitiveness.

Opposition Movements

Conversely, several grassroots movements strongly oppose Project 2025, driven by progressive values and concerns about social justice, environmental protection, and economic equality. Key opposition movements include:

Environmental and Climate Activist Groups

Environmental and climate activist groups, such as the Sierra Club and Greenpeace, strongly oppose Project 2025's environmental policies. These groups advocate for more aggressive action on climate change, increased investment in renewable energy, and stronger environmental regulations. They mobilize public support through campaigns, protests, and advocacy efforts.

Civil Rights and Social Justice Organizations

Civil rights and social justice organizations, including the NAACP and the ACLU, oppose Project 2025's social and cultural policies. These groups advocate for the protection of civil rights, gender equality, and LGBTQ+ rights. They work to raise awareness, influence public opinion, and advocate for policies that promote social justice and equality.

Labor Unions and Worker Advocacy Groups

Labor unions and worker advocacy groups, such as the AFL-CIO and Fight for $15, oppose Project 2025's economic policies. These groups advocate for workers' rights, higher wages, and stronger labor protections. They mobilize public support through strikes, demonstrations, and advocacy campaigns.

Mobilization and Impact

The mobilization efforts of both supportive and opposition grassroots movements significantly impact the public discourse and the potential success of Project 2025.

Public Awareness and Education

Grassroots movements play a crucial role in raising public awareness and educating citizens about Project 2025's policies. Supportive movements work to highlight the benefits and rally support, while opposition movements focus on raising awareness about the potential harms and advocating for alternative approaches. Through community meetings, public forums, social media campaigns, and other outreach efforts, these movements engage and inform the public.

Advocacy and Lobbying

Both supportive and opposition movements engage in advocacy and lobbying efforts to influence policymakers and shape legislative outcomes. These efforts include direct lobbying of elected officials, participating in public hearings, and submitting policy recommendations. Grassroots movements often collaborate with advocacy organizations and think tanks to amplify their impact and ensure their voices are heard.

Electoral Influence

Grassroots movements also exert significant influence during elections. Supportive movements work to mobilize voters in favor of candidates who endorse Project 2025's policies, while opposition movements aim to elect candidates who advocate for alternative approaches. Voter mobilization efforts, such as voter registration drives, canvassing, and get-out-the-vote campaigns, play a crucial role in shaping electoral outcomes.

Protests and Demonstrations

Protests and demonstrations are another powerful tool used by grassroots movements to express their support or opposition to Project 2025. Supportive movements may organize rallies and events to show solidarity and build momentum, while opposition movements may stage protests and demonstrations to raise awareness and pressure policymakers to reconsider specific policies.

Chapter 10: The Path Forward

Potential Challenges and Opportunities

As Project 2025 progresses from conception to implementation, it will inevitably encounter a range of challenges and opportunities. Understanding these potential hurdles and leveraging opportunities will be crucial for ensuring the success and longevity of the initiative.

Challenges

Political Polarization and Partisanship

One of the most significant challenges facing Project 2025 is the high level of political polarization and partisanship in the United States. The initiative's ambitious reforms are likely to face opposition from those with differing political views, making it difficult to achieve consensus and pass legislation. Bridging the partisan divide and finding common ground will be essential for advancing Project 2025's goals.

Economic Inequality

Addressing economic inequality while implementing tax cuts and deregulation is a complex challenge. Critics argue that these policies may disproportionately benefit the wealthy and exacerbate income disparities. Project 2025 must find ways to ensure that its economic policies promote broad-based prosperity and address the needs of low- and middle-income Americans.

Environmental Concerns

Environmental activists and organizations are likely to oppose aspects of Project 2025's energy policies, particularly those that emphasize increased fossil fuel production and nuclear energy. Balancing the need for energy independence with environmental sustainability will be a critical challenge. Project 2025 must demonstrate a commitment to addressing climate change and promoting renewable energy.

Social and Cultural Resistance

Social and cultural policies aimed at preserving traditional values may face resistance from progressive groups and advocates for civil rights, gender equality, and LGBTQ+ rights. Ensuring that these policies do not undermine the progress made in these areas will be essential for maintaining social cohesion and protecting individual freedoms.

Global Geopolitical Dynamics

Navigating the complex and evolving global geopolitical landscape presents another significant challenge. Rival powers such as China and Russia will continue to assert their influence, potentially leading to conflicts and strategic tensions. Project 2025 must develop robust foreign policy and national security strategies to address these challenges and maintain American leadership.

Implementation and Bureaucratic Hurdles

Implementing the wide-ranging reforms outlined in Project 2025 will require navigating bureaucratic hurdles and ensuring effective coordination among various government agencies. Streamlining processes, ensuring accountability, and overcoming resistance within the bureaucracy will be critical for successful implementation.

Opportunities

Economic Growth and Innovation

Project 2025's focus on tax reform, deregulation, and promoting free enterprise presents significant opportunities for economic growth and innovation. By creating a more favorable business environment, the initiative can spur investment, create jobs, and drive technological advancements, positioning the United States as a global leader in innovation.

Energy Independence and Security

Achieving energy independence through increased domestic energy production and investment in renewable energy presents a major opportunity for enhancing national security and economic stability. Reducing reliance on foreign energy sources can mitigate geopolitical risks and ensure a stable energy supply.

Strengthening National Defense

Investing in military readiness, modernizing defense capabilities, and addressing emerging threats provides opportunities to strengthen national defense and maintain global leadership. Project 2025's emphasis on cybersecurity, space capabilities, and advanced technologies can enhance the military's effectiveness and resilience.

Advancing Social and Economic Mobility

Policies aimed at workforce development, education reform, and supporting small businesses can promote social and economic mobility. By providing individuals with the skills and opportunities needed to succeed, Project 2025 can help reduce inequality and create a more inclusive economy.

Building Strong Alliances

Strengthening diplomatic relations and international alliances presents opportunities to address global challenges collaboratively. By building strong partnerships with allies, Project 2025 can enhance collective security, promote democratic values, and address issues such as climate change and global health.

Community and Civic Engagement

Promoting community-based adaptation to climate change and supporting civic engagement can strengthen social cohesion and empower individuals to participate in the political process. Project

2025 can foster a sense of shared responsibility and collective action to address common challenges.

Long-Term Vision and Goals

Project 2025 is not just a set of policies but a comprehensive vision for the future of American governance. Its long-term goals and objectives are designed to ensure that the United States remains a prosperous, secure, and democratic nation.

Sustaining Economic Prosperity

Innovation and Competitiveness

One of the primary long-term goals of Project 2025 is to sustain economic prosperity by fostering innovation and maintaining global competitiveness. This involves continuous investment in research and development, support for emerging technologies, and policies that promote entrepreneurship and free enterprise. By staying at the forefront of technological advancements, the United States can ensure long-term economic growth and job creation.

Inclusive Growth

Ensuring that economic growth benefits all Americans is another key objective. Project 2025 aims to create an inclusive economy where individuals from all backgrounds have access to opportunities and can achieve economic mobility. This includes addressing barriers to education, providing workforce training, and supporting small businesses and entrepreneurship.

Enhancing National Security

Modernized Military Capabilities

Maintaining a modern and capable military is essential for long-term national security. Project 2025's vision includes continuous investment in advanced technologies, cybersecurity, and space capabilities. By ensuring that the military is prepared to address emerging threats, the initiative aims to protect American interests and maintain global leadership.

Strategic Alliances

Building and maintaining strong strategic alliances is another critical goal. Project 2025 emphasizes the importance of international cooperation and collaboration to address global security challenges. Strengthening alliances with key partners and participating in multilateral organizations are essential for promoting stability and collective security.

Promoting Social Cohesion and Justice

Equal Opportunities

Promoting social cohesion and justice is a core component of Project 2025's long-term vision. This includes ensuring equal opportunities for all individuals, regardless of race, gender, or socioeconomic status. Policies aimed at reducing inequality, protecting civil rights, and promoting social justice are central to creating a more inclusive and equitable society.

Cultural and Social Values

Preserving cultural and social values while respecting diversity and individual freedoms is another important goal. Project 2025 aims to create a society where traditional values are upheld, but progress and innovation are embraced. Balancing these elements is essential for maintaining social harmony and fostering a sense of national identity.

Environmental Sustainability

Climate Resilience

Addressing climate change and promoting environmental sustainability are key components of Project 2025's long-term vision. This includes implementing mitigation and adaptation strategies to reduce greenhouse gas emissions, enhance infrastructure resilience, and protect public health. By promoting renewable energy and sustainable practices, the initiative aims to create a more sustainable future.

Natural Resource Conservation

Protecting and conserving natural resources is another critical objective. Project 2025 emphasizes the importance of sustainable land use, habitat restoration, and biodiversity conservation. By promoting responsible environmental stewardship, the initiative aims to ensure that natural resources are preserved for future generations.

Conclusion: The Future of Democracy and Leadership in America

Project 2025 represents a bold and comprehensive vision for the future of American governance. Its focus on economic prosperity, national security, social cohesion, and environmental sustainability reflects a commitment to addressing the complex challenges facing the nation. As we look to the future, several key themes emerge as central to the success of Project 2025 and the broader trajectory of American democracy and leadership.

Commitment to Democratic Values

At the heart of Project 2025 is a commitment to democratic values and principles. This includes protecting individual freedoms, promoting the rule of law, and ensuring equal representation. Upholding these values is essential for maintaining the legitimacy and stability of democratic institutions. By fostering civic engagement and promoting transparency and accountability in governance, Project 2025 aims to strengthen the foundations of American democracy.

Embracing Innovation and Adaptation

The ability to innovate and adapt is crucial for addressing the dynamic challenges of the 21st century. Project 2025 emphasizes the importance of continuous investment in research and development, support for emerging technologies, and the promotion of entrepreneurship. By embracing innovation and fostering a culture of adaptability, the initiative aims to ensure that the United States remains a global leader in economic and technological advancements.

Fostering Social and Economic Equity

Creating a more inclusive and equitable society is a central goal of Project 2025. This includes addressing economic disparities, protecting civil rights, and promoting social justice. By ensuring that all individuals have access to opportunities and can achieve economic mobility, the initiative aims to build a more cohesive and just society. Policies that support education, workforce development, and small businesses are essential for achieving this goal.

Ensuring Environmental Sustainability

Environmental sustainability is critical for the long-term health and prosperity of the nation. Project 2025's commitment to addressing climate change, promoting renewable energy, and protecting natural resources reflects a recognition of the interconnectedness of environmental and economic health. By implementing comprehensive environmental policies and promoting sustainable practices, the initiative aims to create a resilient and sustainable future.

Strengthening National and Global Security

Maintaining national and global security is essential for protecting American interests and promoting stability. Project 2025's focus on modernizing military capabilities, enhancing cybersecurity, and building strategic alliances reflects a commitment to addressing emerging threats and ensuring collective security. By fostering international cooperation and participating in multilateral organizations, the initiative aims to create a more stable and secure world.

The Future of American Leadership

As the United States navigates the complex and evolving landscape of the 21st century, the principles and policies outlined in Project 2025 provide a roadmap for ensuring continued leadership and prosperity. By balancing economic growth with environmental sustainability, promoting social and economic equity, and upholding democratic values, the initiative aims to create a future where all Americans can thrive.

The success of Project 2025 will depend on the ability to navigate challenges, leverage opportunities, and build consensus across diverse perspectives. By fostering collaboration, promoting innovation, and ensuring accountability, the initiative can create a foundation for a prosperous, secure, and democratic future.

As we move forward, it is essential to remain vigilant and proactive in addressing the challenges and opportunities that lie ahead. By staying true to the principles of democracy, embracing innovation, and promoting equity and sustainability, Project 2025 can help ensure that the United States remains a beacon of leadership and a force for positive change in the world.

Conclusion

"Project 2025: Understanding the Future of Democracy and America's Mandate for Conservative Leadership" offers a comprehensive vision for the future of American governance. The book outlines the essential principles and policies necessary to address contemporary challenges while maintaining the core values that have historically defined the nation.

The purpose of this book is to provide a detailed roadmap for policymakers, citizens, and stakeholders who seek to understand and implement the conservative vision for America's future. By examining economic policies, national security strategies, social justice initiatives, and environmental and energy plans, the book presents a holistic approach to governance that aims to promote prosperity, security, and sustainability.

The value of this book lies in its thorough analysis and forward-looking perspective. It emphasizes the importance of innovation and adaptability in navigating the dynamic challenges of the 21st century. By advocating for policies that foster economic growth, protect individual liberties, and promote social and environmental equity, "Project 2025" seeks to build a more inclusive and resilient society.

Through extensive exploration of key topics, including education and healthcare reforms, national security, and diplomatic relations, the book provides actionable insights and practical solutions. It underscores the necessity of balancing economic progress with environmental stewardship and social justice with economic opportunity.

Ultimately, "Project 2025" serves as a vital resource for anyone interested in the future of American democracy. It encourages readers to engage in the political process, advocate for policies that reflect their values, and work collaboratively towards a prosperous, secure, and equitable future. By understanding the proposed policies and their implications, citizens can make informed decisions and contribute to shaping the future of the nation. This book aims to inspire and guide the next generation of leaders, policymakers, and engaged citizens committed to advancing the ideals of democracy and leadership in America.

Thank You

Thank you for choosing to read "Project 2025: Understanding the Future of Democracy and America's Mandate for Conservative Leadership." I sincerely appreciate your time and effort in exploring the ideas and policies presented in this book.

Your decision to select this book among many others is truly valued. I hope the insights and perspectives provided here have been informative and thought-provoking. Your engagement with this material plays a crucial role in the ongoing dialogue about the future of our nation.

If you found this book helpful, I would be grateful if you could take a moment to leave a review. Your feedback is invaluable and helps other readers discover and benefit from the content as well. Thank you once again for your support and for being a part of this important conversation.

Warm regards,